BAKING YOUR WAY TO THE TOP

Companion Workbook

How to Start and Grow Your Own Home-Based Baking Business

Nicole Bendig-Lamb

For more information, email
nicole@cakebusinessschool.com

Photo credit to Samantha Markey Photography

979-8-21833-300-3 - paperback

DISCLAIMER

ACCURACY OF INFORMATION

While reasonable effort has been made to furnish accurate and up-to-date information, information provided in this book is not warranted to be accurate, complete, reliable, up-to-date, or error-free. We assume no liability or responsibility for any errors or omissions in the content of this website or such other materials or communications.

ADVICE is NOT PROVIDED

The information contained within this book is provided for informational purposes only and is not intended as a substitute for obtaining accounting, tax, or other financial advice from your professional accountant. Presentation of the information via the Internet is not intended to create, and receipt does not constitute, an accountant-client relationship. Readers of this site are advised not to act upon this information without seeking the service of a professional accountant.

DISCLAIMER of WARRANTIES and LIMITATIONS of LIABILITY

This book is provided on an "as is" and "as available" basis. Use of this boo is at your own risk. We and our suppliers disclaim all warranties. Neither we nor our suppliers shall be liable for any damages of any kind due to the use of this website.

LINKS TO EXTERNAL THIRD PARTY WEBSITES

For your convenience, this book may contain hyperlinks to websites and servers maintained by third parties. We do not control, evaluate, endorse or guarantee content found on those sites. We do not assume any responsibility or liability for the actions, products, services and content of these sites or the parties that operate them. Your use of such sites is entirely at your own risk.

Table of Contents

Congratulations on investing in yourself!

This workbook is the ultimate companion to my best-selling book, 'Baking Your Way to The Top.'

It's filled with actionable items and practical exercises, making it easier than ever to implement the strategies and tips covered in the book.

Get ready to elevate your baking game and unleash your full potential in the kitchen!

Happy Baking!

Start Your Cake Business: 10 Steps

Step 1: Get Legal

Food License or Cottage Foods Compliance

Before starting your cake or baking business make sure that you are operating according to your local jurisdictions for selling baked goods. *The guidelines provided here are not a substitution for your own research into rules that apply to your area or country, but intended to help you find the information and resources you need.*

The first thing that you will need to do is **see if you are required to have a food service license**, a **commercial kitchen**, or if your area allows food to be sold from a **home kitchen (in the US this is known as Cottage Foods Compliance).**

Each state in the US has different rules for the sale of food, but more states than ever have adopted the **Cottage Foods Act, which allows certain types of food items to be sold from a home kitchen..**

For example, I operate in the **State of Colorado,** and their information on Cottage Foods can be found at this link: **https://cdphe.colorado.gov/cottage-foods-act**

Helpful Links/Searches:
United States: Cottage Food Policy, you can do a quick Google search for "Cottage Foods Law in [insert your State Name Here]."
United States: Retail Food Service licensing, Google search for "Food Service Licensing in [insert your State Name   Here]."
United Kingdom: https://www.food.gov.uk/business-guidance/starting-a-food-business-from-home
Canada: https://www.foodsafety.ca/blog/how-open-food-business-canada
Australia: https://www.foodstandards.gov.au/foodsafety/standards/Pages/Home-based-food-businesses.aspx
All other areas of the world: Google search for "food license requirements in [insert your city or town name]"

Food License or Cottage Foods Compliance cont.

Most governing agency websites for food service have FAQs and easy-to-read guidelines for new businesses.

Make sure that you also **check with all local jurisdictions at each level of government for where you live.** For example, I live in the State of Colorado, but I also reside in a county and city, so I had to make sure that I checked with ALL of these agencies to make sure I'm fully compliant.

Other things that *may* be required for food licensing:

- Register a business name
- Pass a Food Service Safety course
- Carry insurance
- Label all food sold with specific verbiage
- Comply with other restrictions (i.e., only sell approved types of food, follow income limits, etc).

Register a Business Name

As mentioned above, you may be required to register a business name for your food service licensing, but I recommend that you do this step regardless. *(If you live in the US this is usually done with your state Secretary of State office and is generally easily completed on line for a very small fee)*

The importance of distinguishing that your business is its own entity is important for several reasons. The first reason is to have a separation from you as an individual to your **business as its own entity which would carry liability protection through insurance etc.**

Another reason to keep your business separate from your personal income and expenses is to **make sure that you do indeed run it like a business, and not an expensive hobby!** We will talk more about this further in the lessons but for bookkeeping purposes, income tax purposes, and liability reasons it is best to not co-mingle your business with your personal accounts etc.

Tax Identification

In addition to registering your business name, you will also need a Tax Identification Number.
This is a number assigned to your business entity which you will use when filing your tax returns and many other documents, including applications for loans or other business purposes.

In the United States this can be set up easily online through the Internal Revenue Service, and in Australia it is called an ABN.

Link for Tax ID in the US: Apply for a US Federal Tax ID #
Link for ABN in Australia: Apply for an ABN Australia

(If you live in another country, Google search for **"how to get a tax identification number in [insert your country name here]"**)

Sales Tax Licensing

Most areas will require you to collect and remit sales tax for goods that you sell. Again you will need to check with YOUR local jurisdictions, but if you check with your state or area's Department of Revenue they should have resources to help you obtain the proper sales tax licensing and instructions on collecting sales tax and remitting your returns and payment.

Insurance

The next part is to set up insurance policies . At the bare minimum, you need to carry **Food Liability and General Business Liability insurance policies.**

Food Liability insurance is to cover you in the rare occasion where a customer gets ill or injured from consuming your goods. For my food liability insurance policy I use FLIP (Click the link for more information) <u>Food Liability Insurance Program.</u>

There are certainly plenty of options for your Food Liability policy needs, so if you don't like what you see from FLIP, you can do a Google search, or even check with your own insurance carrier as most larger companies offer policies like this.

General Business Liability offers an additional layer of protection in case of lawsuits that may arise from everyday business activities. It can help cover things like:

- Third-party bodily injury
- Third-party property damage
- Product liability
- Advertising injuries (like libel, slander and copyright)

I obtained my general business liability from my insurance carrier. You can either ask an agent with whom you already work, or do a Google search for "General Business Liability Insurance" to find more resources.

Step 2: Decide on a Bookkeeping System
Bookkeeping System - Spreadsheets or Accounting Software?

Bookkeeping is essential to having a profitable and successful business. Things to know about bookkeeping:

- It should be **started from the very beginning**
- It should be **kept up to date** (at least twice a month but weekly is better).
- You **don't have to have any fancy software**. (You can start out with a simple excel spreadsheet - templates available in your course).
- You **can also use online accounting software** applications like
  - QuickBooks Online
  - Freshbooks
  - Xero
  - Or many other platforms.
  - I personally use a **desktop version of QuickBooks**, but this is mostly because I used to be an accountant and already owned the software! No reason to set up something new when I already had that in place.

If you've already got something you can use, don't reinvent the wheel, but also **don't skip this step!**

Step 3: Website
Website for your Cake Business

Having a website, even a basic one to start, **is also essential** to having a profitable and successful business.

Things to consider:
- Free or Low-cost DIY type? Some options are:
  - Wix
  - GoDaddy
  - Squarespace
  - I also recommend BiziBakes
- Mid-range cost DIY type?
  - WordPress
  - Bluehost
- Higher cost option hire a professional?
  - Custom-built website companies

Scan to visit BiziBakes

You have some options on how you want to proceed with having a website. But don't overcomplicate it. Just have one!

I can tell you that I started my baking business with a DIY very simple website that I designed myself and it worked just fine until my business started to grow.

Then when I really wanted to stand out and have a higher end website, I hired a professional to really showcased my talent! (see link above).

The main thing is to have an easy place where your customers can find you, learn about you, and see some of your awesome work. Like I said, **don't overcomplicate it**. Just get one set up. **Do it now!**

Step 4: Order Business Cards

Business Cards for your Cake Business

Having business cards to hand out is an easy way to get your name out there.

You c**an easily design nice looking business cards yourself** on lots of different platforms.
I absolutely love **Canva** for all my marketing materials! I can drop in my logo all my information and within minutes have a really nice designed business card that I can either order to be printed directly from canva.com or I can upload it to another printing service.

Some other DIY options are:

- Vistaprint.com
- Youprint.com
- Gotprint.com

You can also **work with a graphic designer** if you want a **higher end option**

At least have a business card at the beginning so that you can hand it out to people when you're talking about your exciting new business. You'll also want to have them at expos, markets and to include with cake and goodie orders.

If a physical business card feels a little too "old school," you can also look into digital business card options. I use and recommend Popl. Visit popl.co for more information.

Later **when you have some really great photos** ,I highly recommend designing a postcard sized piece of marketing material that you can keep in your bag or purse to hand out in place of a business card. **I love doing this when I really want people to see more than just my logo and maybe one picture.**

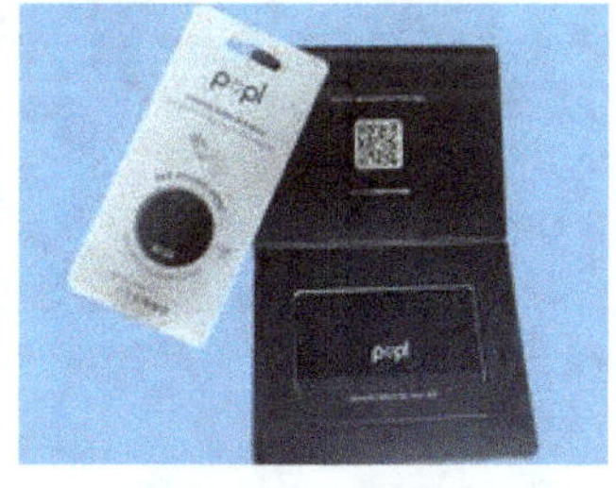

Step 5: Get Customers
Getting Customers and Sharing Your New Business!

This step is going to be discussed even more in the **marketing module**, but you just need a starting point.

Most of us are thinking about starting a cake business because **we've already been baking for friends and family** and now we have **people asking us if they can buy baked goods from us**. Those are your first customers! Ask them to spread the word about your amazing goodies and build your network from there.

Some other ideas to get some business include:

- Flyers
- Join local Facebook groups (like neighborhoods, etc.)
- Join networking groups

Really the biggest part of this step is to get used to the fact that you are **now open for business!** Since you can't sell a secret, you need to let your potential customers know this.

This will get easier and you'll refine your target market, but up front you need to share that that you are taking orders!

Step 6: Pricing for Profit

Pricing for Profit

Pricing is probably the most difficult thing for all bakers when they start out. But it doesn't have to be that hard!

You we'll go through a basic pricing training in this course which includes:

- A cake pricing calculator (to help you cost out your recipes for a specific Gross Profit Margin (GPM) percentage.
- Training on what GPM % is an what you should shoot for in your baking business to start out.

At cake Business School we are also a Profit First certified school, so we highly recommend that you grab the book Profit First by Mike Michalowicz and if you would like further guidance on how to implement Profit First in your baking business you can reach out for a profit assessment and other training on this method.

Step 7: Attend Events

Get Your Name Out There!

One of the best ways to get your name out there is to **have a vendor booth** at events such as markets, expos, and festivals in your local area.

- I started out by having a booth at a local farmers market to sell cupcakes and cookies on site while getting the word out about my amazing custom cakes.
- I also talk a lot about joining networking groups. The best thing that I did for my business was to join my local Chamber of Commerce. They provide lots of resources for small business owners and plenty of networking activities to meet other business owners in and out of your industry and it just opens up lots of doors for exposure.

Step 8: Give Out Samples

Give Out Samples

Another way to let people know about you is to **provide samples.**

You can do this in many different ways by having small containers of **mini cupcakes, cake pops, or cookies.** Take them into local businesses with **business cards** give **vouchers or coupons** with a limited deal.

When I used to work in an office I always loved it when someone popped by with free food!

Step 9: Social Media Presence

Social Media For Your Cake Business

Having a social media presence for your business is essential, but the biggest piece of advice I can give you is to think about where your target market is hanging out?

- I use a **Facebook** business page for a lot of my cake business marketing
- I also have an **Instagram** and **Pinterest** presence as well.

So **where are YOUR perfect customers** hanging out? Do you think they are on Facebook then definitely have a Facebook business page. Maybe they are more the Instagram type? Jump on there.

I have found that **Facebook** and **Instagram** are my two biggest places where I get business from people who might not know me otherwise.

Step 10: Try, Test, Tweak, Repeat!

Try, Test, Tweak, Repeat!

Do Steps 1-9 over and over again until you find the right flavor for your cake or baking business!

To get the most out of it, I recommend that you keep a journal so that you know the following:

- What worked?
- What didn't work?
- Am I attracting the right kind of customers? If not, what can I change to refine this?
- Does my menu reflect my true passion and talents?
- Am I making a profit?

Remember, what isn't measured, can't be improved!

Getting Clear on Your Business Intentions

STEP 1 - ANSWER THE FOLLOWING QUESTIONS (KEEPING IN MIND YOUR CAKE BUSINESS DREAMS)

WHAT MAKES YOU HAPPY? WHAT DO YOU LOVE DOING?

WHAT HAVE BEEN YOUR MOST ENJOYABLE ACHIEVEMENTS IN YOUR BUSINESS SO FAR?

IF YOU COULD DO, BE OR HAVE ANYTHING IN YOUR BUSINESS, WHAT WOULD YOU CHOOSE?

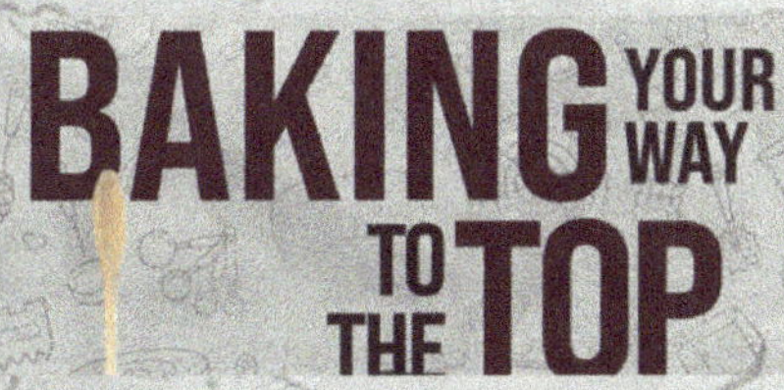

STEP 2 - READ THROUGH YOUR STEP 1 ANSWERS AND HIGHLIGHT WORDS & PHRASES THAT JUMP OUT TO YOU. (FOR EXAMPLE, DO YOU NOTICE COMMON THEMES?)

WRITE SOME OF THE WORDS OR PHRASES THAT FEEL IMPORTANT TO YOU:

USE THE ABOVE WORDS AND PHRASES TO HELP YOU COME UP WITH YOUR **"BIG PICTURE DREAM"** FOR YOUR CAKE BUSINESS!

(We will break this down farther in subsequent lessons)

Example:
Common words/phrases: children's cakes, making kids happy, sharing my knowledge, having an impact.
Big picture dream: To have a baking business where I can focus on creating cakes specifically for kids and where I can offer instruction for young aspiring bakers.

S M A R T

SPECIFIC **MEASURABLE** **ACTION ORIENTED** **RESULTS-BASED RELEVANT** **TIMELY**

Specific: Be as specific as possible (why, what, when, where, how)

Measurable: is the goal measured (from and to) by tracking the progress and measure of the outcome

Action-oriented: by doing what will you achieve the result?

Results-based/Relevant: What result are you looking to achieve? Is it relevant by fitting in to your long-term plans?

Timely: Your goal should include a time limit or deadline

"All who have accomplished great things have had a great aim, have fixed their gaze on a goal which was high, one which sometimes seemed impossible."

--Orison Swett Marden

"Our goals can only be reached through a vehicle of a plan, in which we must fervently believe, and upon which we must vigorously act. There is no other route to success."

--Pablo Picasso

"All successful people have a goal. No one can get anywhere unless he knows where he wants to go and what he wants to be or do."

--Norman Vincent Peale

Here are some examples of goals rewritten as SMART Goals

GOAL: I want to earn more money.

SMART GOAL: I want to increase my net profit from $20,000 to $30,000 for the financial year.

GOAL: I want to earn more money.

SMART GOAL: I want to increase average sale from $150 to $250 and a minimum of 3 orders per week, within 3 months, by October 1, 20xXX I want to be fully booked out (approx. 6 orders averaging $200), within 6 months by December 31, 20XX.

GOAL: I want to earn more money.

SMART GOAL: I want to increase my GPM from 20% to 60% within 6 months by December 31, 20XX. I want to increase GPM from 20% to 40% within 3 months by October 20XX.

GOAL: I want to have a storefront bakery.

SMART GOAL: I want to have a shop front within 2.5 years, by December 20XX. I want to increase my GPM from 20% to 60% by December 31, 20XX, increase monthly sales from $1000 to $4000 per month by December 31, 20XX.

SMART Goals Exercise

So, think back on your big picture plans. Are your goals SMART?
Let's smarten them up! (*We will explore this further in the next Module*)

Use the space below to rewrite your intentions as a goal, and then, as SMART goals.

1. Intention/Goal

SMART Goal

2. Intention/Goal

SMART Goal

3. Intention/Goal

SMART Goal

"The best way to get started is to quit talking and begin doing."
--Walt Disney

Overcoming Limiting Beliefs

WHAT IS A 'LIMITING BELIEF'?

A limiting belief is a state of mind, opinion, or thought that you *think* to be true & that limits you in some way. *"I can't do X, because of Y"*

Here are two examples of limiting beliefs that I personally had, and subsequently overcame!

Personal limiting belief:

"I'll never marry again because I've had my heart broken too deeply." (I just celebrated TEN years with the absolute love of my life!)

Business limiting belief:

"I could never have a fulltime cake business because I would never make enough money." (Two years ago I was able to quit my day job and now run my own <u>successful cake business</u>)

STARTING WITH YOUR THOUGHTS ABOUT **HAVING YOUR OWN CAKE BUSINESS**, WRITE DOWN YOUR TOP 5 *LIMITING BELIEFS:
Refer to the "List of Common Limiting Beliefs" for help

List of Common Limiting Beliefs

Old Belief		New Power Slogan
"I am a failure"	1.	"I learn from every experience and I never give up!"
"Things never work out for me"	2.	"Opportunities are all around me!"
"I'm not talented enough"	3.	"I have amazing gifts & talents that are unique to me!"
"I don't have what it takes"	4.	"I can accomplish anything I set my mind to. What one can do, another can do!"
"It's impossible to make money doing what you love"	5.	"I don't have to choose between money & my passion. I can do both!"
"Money never comes to me easily"	6.	"Money flows to me effortlessly!"
"I never have enough money"	7.	"I manage my money because when I do, more money comes my way!"
"Money doesn't grow on trees"	8.	"There's enough money for everyone who is willing to earn it!"
"Money is the root of all evil"	9.	"Money is a resource to do good in my life and for others!"
"I have to work hard for money"	10	"I do what I love, I solve problems for others & make a large profit"

NOW WITH YOUR THOUGHTS ABOUT **MONEY**, WRITE DOWN YOUR TOP 5 *LIMITING BELIEFS:

Refer to the "List of Common Limiting Beliefs" help

1.

2.

3.

4.

5.

Now for each of the business & money limiting beliefs you've identified, put them through the following steps:

STEP 1 - ARE THEY FACT OR BELIEF? EXPOSE THE DECEPTION

Just because someone believes something, doesn't make it true. Think about things people used to accept as FACT but we now know they were FALSE beliefs:

- The Earth is flat!
- Mercury as a medical treatment!
- Radium is good for you!

STEP 2 - WHICH ONES ARE HOLDING YOU BACK THE MOST?

Highlight your top 2 or 3 that you think are keeping you from reaching your goals.

STEP 3 - TIME TO FLIP THE SCRIPT!

Holding onto these beliefs hasn't served you well in the past and in order to push through them, you must first **identify them**, **acknowledge them** and **be ready to change them!** For each of your top limiting beliefs, re-write them as a new mantra or power slogan that you can repeat to yourself each time that inner critic voice pipes up!

TIME TO RE-WRITE YOUR TOP LIMITING BELIEFS AS YOUR NEW POWER SLOGANS!

Business Limiting Beliefs

1. Old Belief

   New Power
   Slogan

2. Old Belief

   New Power
   Slogan

3. Old Belief

   New Power
   Slogan

Money Limiting Beliefs

1. Old Belief

   New Power
   Slogan

2. Old Belief

   New Power
   Slogan

3. Old Belief

   New Power
   Slogan

Suggested Reading List

Playing Big
by Tara Mohr

In <u>Playing Big</u>, Tara Mohr offers you the keys to unlocking your gifts, your potential and your power to make a difference.

My take-away: I found that her exercises on identifying your inner critic AND your inner mentor to be extremely helpful!

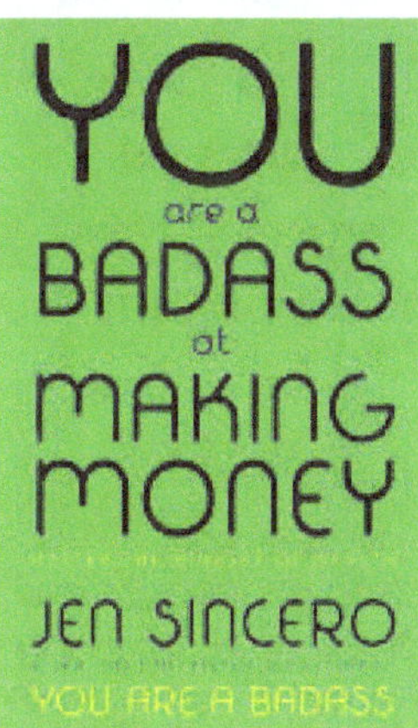

You Are A Badass At Making Money
by Jen Sincero

<u>You Are a Badass at Making Money</u> will launch you past the fears and stumbling blocks that have kept financial success beyond your reach.

My take-away: I listened to this book on Audible LITERALLY 3 times in a row!! I love it and the concepts are empowering to help you get past your blocks about money.

Happy Money
by Ken Honda

<u>Happy Money</u> is written by Japan's #1 bestselling personal development guru. He teaches you how to achieve peace of mind when it comes to money

My take-away: This book helped me uncover a lot of my unhealthy beliefs around money and also emphasizes the importance of gratitude.

Lifestyle Congruence

WHAT IS LIFESTYLE CONGRUENCE?

Lifestyle congruence is a concept introduced by Mike Michalowicz in his book, <u>Fix This Next.</u> It refers to answering the following question: Do you know what your business sales need to be to support your personal comfort?

Determining this amount is really the first step that should be performed before filling out your business plan. It may seem silly, but many business owners focus so much on setting an arbitrary sales goal (out the blue), instead of thinking it through at the level that will personally effect them the most.

Instead, it's better to start with analyzing what your necessary take home pay *needs* to be, and then reverse engineer this back to your top line sales.

This may sound like a difficult and mysterious process, but it's pretty simple, really!

We will go through a process called a **Lifestyle Congruence Evaluation** to get this going.

HOW MUCH IN CAKE / BAKING SALES DO I NEED TO BRING IN TO SUPPORT MY PERSONAL COMFORT?

1. Add up your monthly living expenses OR the amount of take-home pay you'd like from your cake business. This is your comfort level, not your dream income (that will come later)! NOTE: Be truly honest with yourself, what could you do without in your personal life to reduce the initial burden to your cake business?

Total:

2. Apply the formula to determine sales revenue needed:

$$\_\_\_\_\_\_\_\_\_\_ \div .35 = \_\_\_\_\_\_\_\_\_\_$$

(Total from Step 1.) **(Sales Revenue Needed)**

3. BONUS step: *If you know at this point what your average cake order price is, you can divide it into the "Sales Revenue Needed" from Step 2 to see how many baking orders you need to meet this goal.

*If you don't know yet what your average cake order price is, don't worry! We will cover this in subsequent lessons!

Business Planning

What isn't measured can't be improved. If you want a profitable business, you need to be measuring and tracking. And that starts with a business plan.

Think of a business plan like New Years Resolutions. We set the intention for the year. A business plan is setting the intention for the business year.

For example, how much money you want to make in the next year. Or what type of business you want. That is all connected.

A business plan is a working document. You don't write it and walk away. It is a constantly evolving document.

It isn't written in stone. Think of it as lead pencil on a piece of paper. It can be changed and updated.

But as long as you have a plan and work towards it (versus no plan and running around like a headless chicken). Your plan is your path. Your journey you are taking.

And the process of writing a business plan starts with looking back. Looking back on the past year, or so far in business and readjusting your path to stay on track.

For a first business plan, you are writing your ideas down.

Business plans needs to be constantly reviewed. Like bookkeeping is constantly updated. Don't let your numbers fall by the way-side and don't let your business plan fall by the way-side.

Schedule in regular business plan reviews. I suggest once per month. In the first week of the month, the month, once you have updated your bookkeeping.

If I ask you, how much did you earn last year? (Either calendar year or financial year.) Do you know the answer? Looking back is as important as looking forward.

How much did you make in the last year? (Either calendar year or financial year.)
- Gross profit
- Total expenses
- Net profit

When I set my income goals, it starts with looking back at the previous year and knowing my numbers, which is powerful. Without knowing my numbers, how can I move or grow (and by how much) if I don't have a starting point? And how will I know if I reach my goal?

For example if I want to increase my profit by 20%, I need to know what profit I made last year and by end of the year I will know if I reach that number?

Don't over think this.
Don't freak out.
If you know the amount, write it down. If you don't know, have a guess-timate.
In gross amount, how much did you earn (IN YOUR BUSINESS) in 2014?

HEADS UP - This exercise you are really *really* don't want to do. (Because that means your book keeping needs to be up to date. And also if you don't know your numbers - your profit/expenses they might come as a surprise.)

BUT, it is important (**trust me**).
What isn't measured can't be improved. And if you are planning on improving your income (and the bottom line - net profit) that ONLY comes from knowing your numbers.

(**Note**– if you didn't have a business last year, so have no numbers to refer to, don't worry! Just know that knowing your numbers is important in business and you want to be tracking your stats and doing book keeping regularly – monthly – to stay on track.)

#1 How much did you make in the last 12 months?

(Either calendar year or financial year)

- Gross profit:

- Total expenses:

- Net profit:

- Profit margins:

(Note– if you didn't have a business last year, so have no numbers to refer to, don't worry! Just know that knowing your numbers is important in business and you want to be tracking your stats and doing book keeping regularly – monthly – to stay on track.)

Look at money

Knowing your income (gross, net) and expenses gives you a starting point (and remember they can be improved, so don't get all Debby Downer on yourself!)

Knowing how much money you made (gross profit), what was the #1 biggest seller? (And #2 #3 #4 #5). Now, unless you sell products off the shelf, I understand if this is a little difficult as each cake order is different, so try finding natural groups or similar sales. Find what (type) of product/ package / way of selling was the most popular!

Look at your diary and see something correlating or connecting or similar about the orders? Whether it was cupcakes, selling wholesale, 2 tier fondant cakes, $500 wedding cakes, themed party packages, cake pops or the farmers market you attend.

For example~
- Boxes of 12 cupcakes (you sold about 5 per week)
- Cakes between $100-200
- Markets (or Wholesale or Custom Cake Orders)

#2 What were your 5 biggest sellers? (Bonus points if you can list them in order!)

-

-

-

-

-

TIP– *Notice your biggest seller(s) and think of the 80/20 rule. Usually our biggest seller brings in 80% of the income and takes 20% of the time. While our little moolah earners bring in 20% income and takes 80% of the time.*

HINT– *this will give you great insight on what to concentrate on this year and what NOT to concentrate on.*

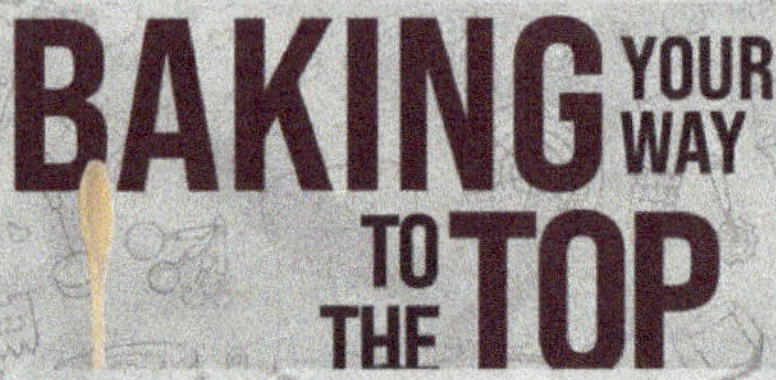

Looking back on the last 12 months – What worked? What didn't?

(We are talking about what 'worked' in the sense of reaching last year's goals, whether it was increasing your email list or for generating income or creating sales or has great profit margins.)

For example did you do a Mother's Day promotion that was popular? Or a market / festival that had great sales? Did you add an opt in to your website? Did you write consistent email newsletters? Was there a marketing strategy that worked (email newsletters, connect with a party coordinator, a giveaway, deal/promo)?

I would love to know–

1. What worked for you?

2. What didn't work for you?

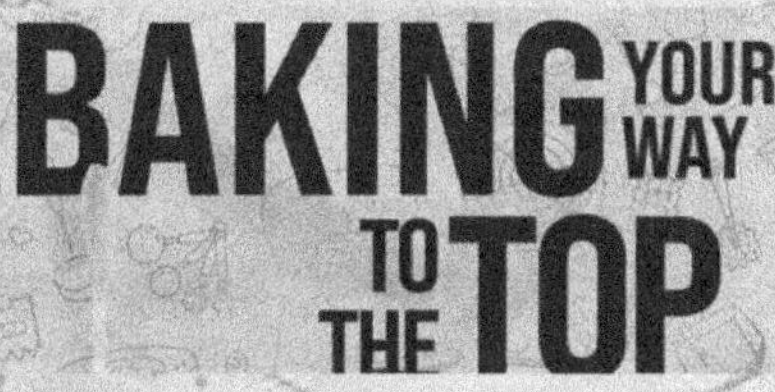

#3 BEFORE getting into the big plans and goals, take a step back. What do you want in the next 12 months?

Sit with that for a moment and jot down on a piece of paper.

Some ideas– switch off Sunday (completely off technology, emails and cooking)
- Work x number of hours
- Increase income (or reduce expenses)
- Go on family holidays
- Supported
- Get a new handbag quarterly!

This is your dream business! What do you want it to look like?

What do you want the next 12 months to LOOK like?

What do you want the next 12 months to FEEL like?

What do you want to GIVE YOURSELF in next 12 months?

#4 What are your BIG PICTURE PLANS? What big ideas and dreams do you have for yourself and your business?

I am talking about Business Goals, in this instance.

For example – do you want to:

- Increase average sale
- Increase email subscriber numbers
- Start your sweet business
- Get a business mentor/coach
- Get a website or update website
- Earn more $
- Increase website hits
- Raise prices
- Blog fortnightly
- Be fully booked out a month in advance

Today, I am only talking about business goals, but there (of course) other types:

(a.) Financial Goals
(b.) Body Goals – loose 4kg, yoga weekly, go fishing
(c.) Family Goals – go on holiday
(d.) Creative Goals
(e.) Spiritual, Friendship and Personal Goals.

Use this page to write down big picture plans for as many as you wish!

Are your goals SMART?

- Specific
- Measurable
- Achievable
- Results (based)
- Timely

Be as SPECIFIC as possible (why, what, when, where, why, how).

- Is the goal MEASURABLE (from and to) by tracking the progress and measure the outcome.

- Is the goal ACHIEVABLE (how) by being reasonable enough to be accomplished?

- Is the goal RELEVANT (worthwhile) by fitting in to your long term plans?

Your goal should by TIMELY (when) and include a time limit (hello, sense of urgency!)

So, think back on your big picture plans. Are your goals SMART? Let's smarten them up!

Examples:

GOAL: I want more email subscribers.

SMART GOAL: I want to increase from 100 email subscribers to 400 by 31 December 20XX.

GOAL: I want to earn more money.

SMART GOAL: I want to increase my net profit from $20K to $30K for the financial year.

GOAL: I want to earn more money.

SMART GOAL: I want to increase average sale from $150 to $250 and a minimum of 3 orders per week, by June 20XX. I want to be fully booked out (approx. 6 orders averaging $200) by 31 December 20XX.

GOAL: I want more website hits.

SMART GOAL: I want to increase av. Monthly website hits from 1000 to 2000 by 31 December 20XX.

Use this page to write down SMART goals

#6 DO IT.

Look at your SMART goals.

- HOW are you going to do it?
- Break it down into mini tasks (again specific and timely).
- Schedule it in.
- Then do the work

Most people get stuck on the HOW. That is when they usually walk away from their goals and not really look back. They might start doing the work, but don't follow through … and why would they! There are too many unanswered questions.

What I do I teach reverse engineering, which is looking at each (1) big business goal and working out the HOW. Together we break down into mini tasks and schedule it in.

THEN (here is the kicker) you need accountability! Someone / s who ask you what is your goal, when are you going to do it and them following up and asking is it done? THAT IS HOW TO GET STUFF DONE! Accountability! You will get it done because you know someone is going to follow up with you.

1-Page Business Plan

biggest sellers: (ex: markets, kids
akes, weddings, other goodies, etc.)

- 1.
- 2.
- 3.

3 best marketing strategies: (ex: WOM,
markets, Facebook, website, etc.)

- 1.
- 2.
- 3.

3 Top Goals for this Year:

- 1.
- 2.
- 3.

Last Month's Income: ___________

Last Year's Income: ___________

This Month's Income: ___________

This Year's Income: ___________

Potential income streams + breakdown

- 1. $
- 2. $
- 3. $

Total:

- 4. $

Marketing: Current Number: Target:

- 1.
- 2.
- 3.

Review Date: _________________ Scheduled? yes / no
Accountability Partner: _________________ Scheduled? yes / no

Pricing Your Cakes – GPM% Method

HOW MUCH SHOULD I CHARGE FOR MY CAKES & BAKED GOODS?
THIS WORKSHEET SHOWS YOU HOW TO USE THE GROSS PROFIT
MARGIN % METHOD OF PRICING

1. Add up all of the direct costs you will incur to make the cake. This includes: ingredients for the cake, filling, frosting, embellishments. This also includes supplies like cake boards, supports, boxes, logo stickers you place on the boxes. Don't leave ANYTHING out! Even 1 teaspoon of sprinkles!!

Total:

2. NOTE: Your DESIRED Gross Profit Margin % should be 50% - 70% in a baking business. You will use this percentage as a decimal in the formula below.

Example: Total costs of $40. Desired GPM% 67%. What is the base price I should charge?

$$\$40 \div (1 - .67) = \$121$$

$$\underline{\qquad\qquad} \div (1 - \text{Desired GPM\%}) = \underline{\qquad\qquad}$$
(Total from Step 1. YOUR COSTS) · (Base Price to Charge)

3. Add any upcharges for additional details, designs or services. Examples include sugar flowers, hand-molded figurines, fondant decorated boards, cake toppers, delivery, etc.

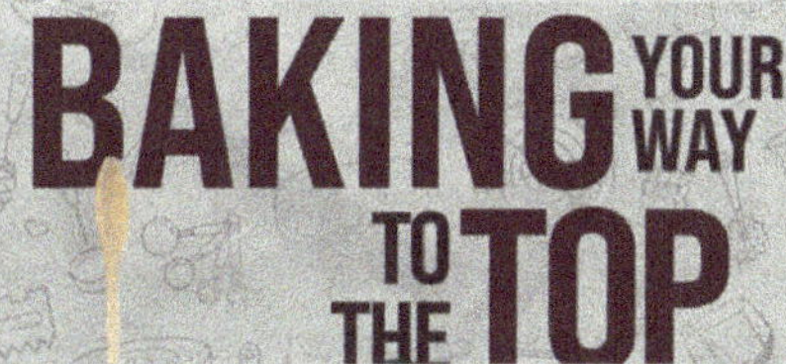

COMPANION WORKBOOK

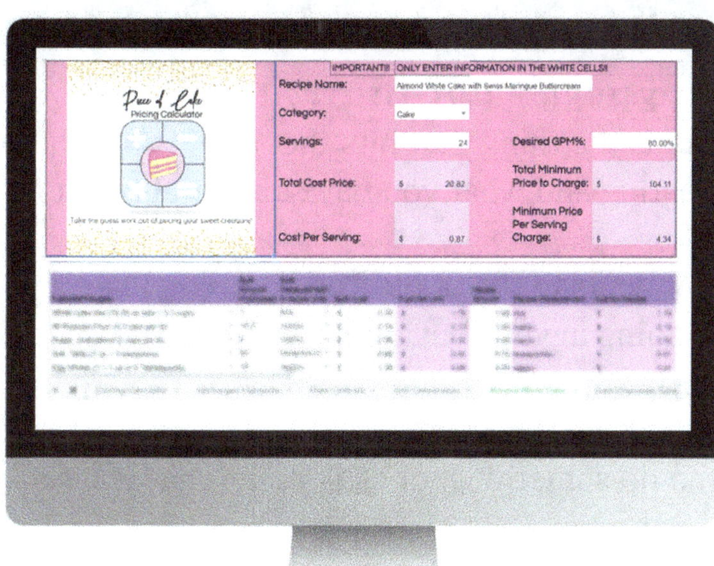

Scan the code below for your copy of The Piece of Cake Pricing Calculator

Identifying your Perfect Product

WHAT IS YOUR PERFECT PRODUCT?

Your perfect product is the thing that hits the "sweet spot" between what you absolutely LOVE creating and what you have a natural talent for!

I talked about the concepts in the book, <u>The Pumpkin Plan</u>, and how straying from what you love doing in your business can limit your success (and quite frankly, burn you out!)

Just because you *can* do something, doesn't mean that you *should.*

My perfect example of this is special diet cakes and desserts. I used to say "yes" to every order type (including these) because I thought that if I said "no," I'd never have any customers. But what I didn't realize was, that if I loaded my schedule up with every order around, then I wouldn't have the time to dedicate to doing the orders or designs that I am really amazing at!

I don't eat special diet cakes, and therefore really know nothing about how to make them well. Saying "yes" to these orders, is doing a disservice to my customers, as well as to my own business!

If we all instead focused on the ONE thing (or few things) that we both 1) love to create, and 2) are GREAT at, can you see how that really serves your customers better?

-EXERCISE

On the following page, COMPARE your favorite types of cakes to make that you identified in the Intentions Module 1 with your best sellers in the Planning Module 2 – do any of these intersect?

There will also be a set of questions that you can ask yourself to help define what **your** best product is.

ist to Compare: Your Favorite Past Orders vs. Your Top Sellers

Favorite Orders   Top Sellers

1.

2.

3.

4.

5.

6.

7.

8.

9.

10.

QUESTIONS TO ASK YOURSELF

Thinking back on past orders or cakes you've made, do you ever think these the following thoughts?

"Yay! I LOVE getting orders for cakes like these!"
What specifically do you like about certain types of orders? Is it the challenge? Is it the way you feel about the finished product? Is it the reaction you get from the customers? Use the space below to jot down some ideas:

____

____

____

How about this:
"Ugh...I HATE these kinds of requests!"
Again, what specifically is it about them that you don't like? Is it that you don't feel passionate about them? Do you feel like it's just not your forte? Do you feel like someone else would enjoy it more? Jot down your thoughts:

____

____

____

PUTTING IT ALL TOGETHER

Now, you've listed your favorites, compared them to your best sellers and gotten really specific about what it is that lights you up (or sucks your energy!), you should be able to write a sentence or paragraph that clearly describes YOUR perfect product!

Below is my example to help you form this:

> I love getting orders for sculpted cakes in Science Fiction or Fantasy genres. I love the challenge of figuring out how to pull them off and I LOVE the surprise and happiness that they bring my customers! I don't enjoy orders for special diet cakes, as I'm really not good at them, and I don't feel like the final product is up to my quality standards. I feel as though there are so many other bakers who are way better (and more passionate about them) than I am. Therefore, my perfect products are unique sculpted cakes in fondant and other 3D edible medium where I can focus my passion on re-creating awe-inspiring designs in Sci Fi, Fantasy and Horror, or Food Realism. These are usually milestone birthday cakes, groom's cakes or retirement cakes.

Now write your perfect product description below:

____

____

____

____

____

Where to find your ideal customers!

HERE ARE A FEW EXAMPLES AND TIPS TO HELP YOU FIND THEM!

YOUR PERFECT PRODUCT IS **WEDDING CAKE** AND YOUR PERFECT CUSTOMER IS A **FIRST-TIME BRIDE**

She's reading local bridal publications, attending bridal expos, asking in Facebook groups about where other brides went for their wedding vendors,

You can:

- Connect with other wedding industry professionals and establish a referral relationship (wedding planners, venues, caterers, florists, photographers, videographers, bridal gown/tux shops, etc.)
- Have a vendor booth at a bridal expo and hold a drawing to win a complimentary box of cupcakes for a shower to collect her name, phone #, email, wedding date, and if she's met with any other cake vendors
- Become a preferred vendor with a wedding or event venue
- Advertise in your local bridal publications

YOUR PERFECT PRODUCT IS **CHILDREN'S BIRTHDAY CAKES** AND YOUR PERFECT CUSTOMER IS A **MOM OF ELEMENTARY AGE KIDS**

She's hanging out at school events, at pick up and drop offs. She hangs out at soccer practice and dance recitals.

You can:

- Advertise in the school newsletters
- Have a vendor booth at school craft shows
- Have a Facebook business page and join mom groups that allow promotional posts
- Connect with other vendors and businesses who cater to children's parties (martial arts studios, kid's party centers, etc.

The basic idea is that if you **know your customer**, then you should be a to figure out **where to find them** and come up with **ways to connect**

Finding Your Perfect Products & Customers Suggested Reading List

The Pumpkin Plan

by Mike Michalowicz

So what is <u>The Pumpkin Plan?</u> Plant the right seeds: Don't waste time doing a bunch of different things just to please your customers. Instead, identify the thing you do better than anyone else and focus all of your attention, money, and time on figuring out how to grow your company doing it.

My take-away: This book was seriously LIFE CHANGING for my business! I don't say that lightly, either. Finding what you do best and then attracting the best customers who appreciate this is a key to not only being successful, but also feeling fulfilled.

The One Thing

by Gary Keller

No matter how success is measured, personal or professional, only the ability to dismiss distractions and concentrate on your ONE Thing stands between you and your goals. <u>The ONE Thing</u> is about getting extraordinary results in every situation.

My take-away: I tend to get really excited about ALL the things (I can tend to have a bit of "shiny object syndrome," but this book helped me see the importance of focusing on the important things and not get distracted by other things that don't move you toward your goals. I find it a great book to read after <u>The Pumpkin Plan.</u>

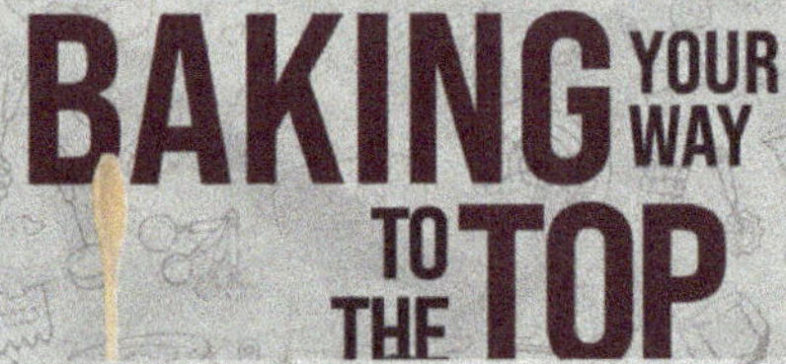

Marketing Plan Template

A marketing action strategy plan is an injection of espresso into your cake business with a step-by-step instructions to kick your business into overdrive. Get your name out there, get inquiries, get clients, get sales, get website traffic and get booked out!

Key Thoughts Before You Begin:
- There are hundreds of marketing strategies and ways to market your business.
- Choosing *which* marketing strategies comes down to you: your preference, personality, your skills set, and what works for you in your business. A strategy that works for me, might not work for you.
- See the attached list of 100 Marketing Tips, as ideas and suggestions to get the ball rolling.
- Remember, whether you have tried it before or not, when you hear the voice inside your head say 'it doesn't work,' turn that around and ask yourself 'how will it work for me!'
- The idea is to start laying marketing strategies, like foundational building blocks. (There is no one magic marketing tactic that is going to get you a million bucks. But multiple marketing and layered strategies is what get results).
- In this marketing plan, I'll start with a selection (personal favs) and - try, test, tweak, repeat
- The only way to know whether it is effective or not is to judge the results (sales), by evaluating the data and sales figures. Then implement additional marketing brick by brick.

Commitment:

I will ask you to make the following commitments:

1. Make the commitment of doing marketing consistently. If you do it inconsistently, then you will have inconsistent results. If you don't market at all you'll get zero results. **Effort in = results out.** Set aside time **DAILY** to be marketing your business and getting sales. This is sales activity or marketing activity and it should be a **priority.**

2. Instead of saying 'this doesn't work for me', change it to say 'HOW can this work for me?' Flip the mindset - on its head. I promise if you think it doesn't work, then it won't.

Say 'HOW can this work for me?'

Key Elements/Steps:

1. Select 3-5 marketing strategies and **commit** to implement these
2. Set your **objectives** in the form of **SMART Goals** (Specific, Measurable, Action-oriented, Results-based, and Time-based)
3. Set your marketing **schedule**: Daily, Weekly, Monthly (consistency is key!)
4. Evaluate your **results**
5. **Tweak and repeat** (or select new strategies)

Step 1: Select Your Strategies (3-5)

Below is a list of some top strategies that are tried and true for baking businesses (*also refer to your "100 Marketing Tips & Strategies" PDF for additional options*):

- **Website**. Have one. If you don't have a website decide: either DIY or get someone else to do it.

- Have a **Facebook business page**. Facebook business page. Post/schedule 3 posts per week. Share from your Facebook business page to your personal page, 3 times per week.

- Join **Facebook groups**. Post once per week into the Facebook group.

- **Vouchers**. Hand out 50-100. Print off vouchers, have in purse ready to give to friends + family, hair salons, even people you strike up conversations with in the grocery store!

- **Samples**. Take samples (I suggest mini cupcakes) + vouchers into shops, hairdresser, clothing, accountant, offices.

- **Markets**. Research and book into at least 1 market. It could be a farmers market, show, expo, festival or event.

- **Monthly birthday register** for sending emails to book cake orders for upcoming parties

- **Email newsletters** – send weekly. Send emails via an email service provider (I use and recommend ConvertKit.)

- **Network** – with wedding planner, party coordinator, wedding receptions, photographers, etc.

Step 2: Set Your Objectives as SMART Goals

Any time that you are spending time, energy (and money) you need to have a very clear objective/goal (result) that you wish to achieve.

Example 1:

From the Monthly Birthday Register, I want 10 birthdays cake orders booked, by the end of June by sending emails twice a month with weekly follow up calls.

Example 2:

Approach cake smash photographers: 3/12/20XX

Create a set price or set guidelines in which the customer can order when they place an order with the photographer. Work with the photographer to create a suitable digital image or flyer for advertising. Make sure I advertise 3x per month on my Facebook page. Make sure I add a flyer to the top of each cake box that is for a kids party.

You will set an objective for EACH marketing Strategy that you picked from Step 1.

Step 3: Set Your Marketing Schedule

Example:

Daily:

1 hour of marketing activities (ex: post in Facebook groups, reach out to other event industry professionals to discuss referring to each other, reach out to past customers for feedback and offer them a quote for upcoming events)

Weekly:

Follow up on quotes

Schedule Facebook business posts

Email Newsletter

Monthly:

Farmers market/expo/show/event

Networking

Monthly birthday register emails

Steps 4 & 5: Evaluate Your Results & Tweak and Repeat

How do you know if your marketing is working?

ROI (Return On Investment) – You need to check whether the money you invested into your marketing strategy is DIRECTLY resulting in a profit. Ex: If you have spent $30.00 on printing Discount Gift Vouchers to hand out at your local Babies & Kids Market – and you have found that this has resulted in $180 worth of orders being placed.

Sales Numbers – This is more specified to your overall marketing plan, rather than individual marketing strategies. You can tell if your sales numbers has increased. Ex: last financial year you earned $26,000, this financial year you earned $38,000

Customer Response/Survey – Ask your customers where they saw your name and why they decided to place an order with you. Collect this information over a certain period of time and review. Ex: After each order is complete, send a customer survey with 2 questions – how satisfied were you with the services, where did you hear about our business?

Because you set clear and measurable objectives/goals in Step 2, this step should be fairly easy to perform.

Looking at the SMART goal you set for each strategy and comparing to your results, you should be able to answer the following questions:

Did I fully meet each part of my goals? If not, did I meet any part?

Which strategies worked?

Which strategies didn't work?

For strategies that partially worked, what can I tweak to try again for better results?

Are there any strategies that didn't work at all that I need to scrap?

What new strategies will I choose to replace any that didn't yield any results?

NOTE: Remember that some strategies may need a longer time to see results than others. This is why you need to evaluate on a weekly basis so that you can keep an eye on your progress.

Marketing Plan Template

Marketing Strategy #1: ________________________________

Objective with SMART criteria [**S**pecific, **M**easurable, **A**ction, **R**esults, **T**ime (deadline)]

____

____

____

____

____

Schedule

Daily Tasks	Weekly Tasks	Monthly Tasks
__________	__________	__________
__________	__________	__________
__________	__________	__________
__________	__________	__________
__________	__________	__________

Evaluate Results   **Date of Review:** ________________

Did I fully meet each part of my goals? Yes/No   If not, did I meet any part? Yes/No

Which part(s) worked: ________________________________

____

____

What can be tweaked to try again for better results? ________________

____

____

Marketing Plan Template

<u>Marketing Strategy #2</u>: _______________________________________

<u>Objective with SMART criteria</u> [**S**pecific, **M**easurable, **A**ction, **R**esults, **T**ime (deadline)]

____

____

____

____

____

<u>Schedule</u>

Daily Tasks	Weekly Tasks	Monthly Tasks
__________	__________	__________
__________	__________	__________
__________	__________	__________
__________	__________	__________
__________	__________	__________

<u>Evaluate Results</u>   **<u>Date of Review:</u>** _______________

Did I fully meet each part of my goals? Yes/No   If not, did I meet any part? Yes/No

Which part(s) worked: _________________________________

____

What can be tweaked to try again for better results? _________________

____

Marketing Plan Template

<u>Marketing Strategy #3</u>: ________________________

<u>Objective with SMART criteria</u> [**S**pecific, **M**easurable, **A**ction, **R**esults, **T**ime (deadline)]

____

____

____

____

____

<u>Schedule</u>

Daily Tasks	Weekly Tasks	Monthly Tasks
_______	_______	_______
_______	_______	_______
_______	_______	_______
_______	_______	_______
_______	_______	_______

<u>Evaluate Results</u>   **<u>Date of Review:</u>** ________________

Did I fully meet each part of my goals? Yes/No   If not, did I meet any part? Yes/No

Which part(s) worked: _______________________________

____

____

What can be tweaked to try again for better results? ________________

____

____

Marketing Plan Template

Marketing Strategy #4: ______________________________________

Objective with SMART criteria [**S**pecific, **M**easurable, **A**ction, **R**esults, **T**ime (deadline)]

____

____

____

____

____

Schedule

Daily Tasks	Weekly Tasks	Monthly Tasks
__________	__________	__________
__________	__________	__________
__________	__________	__________
__________	__________	__________
__________	__________	__________

Evaluate Results   **Date of Review:** _______________

Did I fully meet each part of my goals? Yes/No   If not, did I meet any part? Yes/No

Which part(s) worked: _______________________________

____

____

What can be tweaked to try again for better results? _______________

____

____

Marketing Plan Template

Marketing Strategy #5: ___________________________________

Objective with SMART criteria [**S**pecific, **M**easurable, **A**ction, **R**esults, **T**ime (deadline)]

____

____

____

____

____

Schedule

Daily Tasks	Weekly Tasks	Monthly Tasks
__________	__________	__________
__________	__________	__________
__________	__________	__________
__________	__________	__________
__________	__________	__________

Evaluate Results   **Date of Review:** ___________

Did I fully meet each part of my goals? Yes/No   If not, did I meet any part? Yes/No

Which part(s) worked: ___________________________________

____

____

What can be tweaked to try again for better results? ___________

____

____

100 Marketing Strategies to try with your perfect customers.

- Make a portfolio of your work.
- Ask previous clients for testimonials. There is nothing more powerful than someone else's recommendation to buy from you.
- Share testimonials on website and social media.
- Share any certificates, qualifications, registrations and licenses to prove your skills.
- Include any evidence of awards you have won within your portfolio (on your website and relevant social media platforms).
- Share any magazine or newspaper clips where you, your business or your cakes have received coverage (that includes online websites and blogs, too.)
- Categorize your portfolio into sections – children's, weddings, cupcakes, etc.
- Network. Go to business sessions or mastermind or networking meetings, you never know who you are going to meet.
- Collab with other people in similar industries. For example – wedding coordinators, party planners, gift shops, etc. Offer commissions for cross-promoting or recommending.
- Enroll in <u>Cake Business School</u> which includes video training + bonuses on how to grow your cake business!

Social Media

- Set up a Facebook Business (or Fan) page.
- Join local Facebook groups and share your weekly deal. (These groups are similar to online community noticeboards).
- Share on your personal Facebook page that you are taking cake orders. Your friends and family will be your biggest supporters!
- Improve your Facebook Business page with an App that collects names and email address.
- Create your own Facebook group for people in your local area. Have a competition inviting people to add their friends. Share you latest creations and sneak peaks and deals regularly. Ask people to comment for engagement
- Pin your cake photos and blog posts to Pinterest. It is where your target market are hanging out that is also a visual gallery or portfolio of your work. Create a Pinterest business account.

Advertise Online

- Advertise on Facebook
- Advertise on Google Ads for Small Business
- Get your business added to the Yelp

Offline Marketing

- Bake mini cupcakes and give to local businesses.
- Make up and print off Vouchers and give to people you meet (Check out chicks, neighbors, people at a BBQ, parents at the soccer game).
- Mail box drop with business card and voucher (either yourself, or ask a couple of friends and pay them in cupcakes!)
- Visit your local YMCA, community or sporting clubs and offer your services.
- Message, text or call friends and family who are having a birthday or party soon.
- Go to Restaurant and Café's with free samples.
- School newsletter advertising.
- Day-care newsletter advertising.
- Network. Connect with other people in your community such as other business owners.

Email Marketing

- Send out regular emails newsletters with deals or specials to create interest.
- Collect email address from website, inquiries, orders and events.
- You can manually add email address to an excel spreadsheet or word document and bcc (blind carbon copy) in on emails or use an email service provider like ConvertKit.
- Collect email address from website traffic (more information below).
- Email out your latest creations, your latest blog post, what market or event you will be at next, what shop stocks your goodies, a deal/voucher/discount/sale, what social media platforms you are on, invite to join your Facebook group, sneak peaks, etc.
- Give a call to action (CTA). For example – get a free quote today, click to read more, press button to join Facebook group, hit reply, etc.

Website

- Have a website to share your portfolio and/or gallery to showcase your work.
- Blog regularly (for Google-ability). By regularly adding blog posts and photos you will get better Google ranking.
- Collect email addresses. Over 98% of people who hit your website will navigate away and not contact you – boo!
- Add an 'opt in' to your website, to give incentive for people to give you their email address.
- Have a call to action (CTA) on every single page of your website – I suggest inviting them to contact you for a free quote today!
- Have good quality photos! No blurry, dark or messy cakes here.

Markets, Expos, Shows, Festivals, Events

- Have a stall at festivals, shows, markets and fairs and give out business cards.
- Sell at the markets and hand out business cards.
- Give away free samples, which invites people to try your goodies, they slow down to look at your table, you have time to say 'I have these on special, these are new flavors this week, feel free to enter competition to win free cupcakes' and they generally walk away with a business card!
- Have a competition! At the end of the table have entry forms and a box, where people put their name and contact details to win something (like a box of cupcakes or a voucher). Give each entrant bonus points for putting family member's birthdates! (Now you can add them to email newsletter list.)
- Have a portfolio on display or photo album (laminated photos hanging off sides of table and marquee worked well for me).
- This is how you become known as the local cake chick. People will recognize your brand.
- Have signage that says "Taking Cake Orders Today!"
- Direct people to look at your website and 'Like' your Facebook page (and any other social media platform you are on).
- Take photos of your stall or stand at the event and share on social media, on your website and for email newsletters.
- Invite customers to take photos and share on social media and tag your business in it!

Wedding Expos

- Exhibit at a wedding expo or fair, with more than 1 display cake. This will expose you to more wedding cake orders. Here is the <u>ultimate wedding expo guide</u>.
- Share your portfolio at the wedding expo (it could be a photo book, a TV set up with photos or videos, a laptop with a slideshow playing or a iPad with a gallery for people to click through.) and get other types of cake orders – like birthday, engagement or baby showers!
- Give away brochures, business cards and samples.
- Hold a competition and collect your own leads and contact details at your booth. Collect contact details of people you meet on the day so you can follow up with them after the event. Partner with businesses, such as a romantic meal for 2 or a massage at a spa for prizes and offer to share the lead list with them.
- Sales- Sales usually don't happen on the day of the event. After the show, follow up. FAST. That could be in the way of a quote or a free taste testing day that you are taking bookings for. Normally it takes 1-3 months to see the orders coming in from the event.

Customer Service

- Provide really great customer service! Customer service can be (and usually is) the key to turning potential customers into paying customers.
- Follow up with every. Single. Inquiry. Until it is a 'no', assume it is a 'yes'. Don't think you are being pushy or salesy, because you are not.
- Initial quote - Provide great customer service. That is important. #1 Give very quick quote.
- People are wanting the price $. You do not want to spend 30 min / 60 min every time someone asks for a quote.
- Follow up with a combination of Facebook message, email, phone call, text message, leave a message, etc. People thank me for following up!
- Don't assume or think that the customer should follow up with you!
- Every quote I give 3 quotes. Every quote I give a very (very) quick quote and then give another 2 options. So then you are offering 3 price points and that way the customer is more likely to find something within their budget.

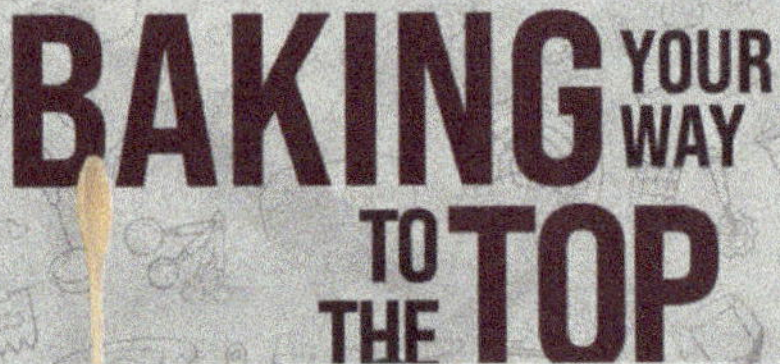

- With each cake order add cake instructions, on how best to delivery, keep and eat the cake with a small handful of business cards (to hand out to friends, family, guests).
- Show confidence (even if you don't feel it), communicate clearly, eye contact and smile.
- WOM! Great customer service and great customer experience equals marketing gold = WOM. Word of mouth is the bees-knees and best marketing tool and strategy for a cake business.
- Offer your previous customers incentive to recommend to friends and family, like a voucher or bonus with their next order (free box of 12 cupcakes, for example.)

What marketing strategies should you use?

Essentially, find what works best for you based on your skill set, personality type, experience, work works for your business and what doesn't.

Remember. Try. Test. Tweak. Repeat.

Collecting Deposits and Having Terms & Conditions (T&C's)

Being in the cake industry, I know all too well myself about dealing with deposits, final payments, cancelled orders and the list goes on. I see very frequently, cakers just starting out, being a little unaware and asking for advice on what they should do in particular circumstances when it comes to customers and money.

I thought I'd write a few tips and advice here from my own personal experience, on how to be firm, polite and professional when it comes to money from customers in the cake industry. You may find that it helps you in the long run.

1. Be Consistent

This is simple. You need to know what your guidelines are for your customers and order process, and be consistent across the board. Whether it's a cake customer, or a family or friend, simply let everybody know the same rules that apply. The deposit is due when? The final payment is due when? How payment can be made?

2. Be Firm, but Flexible

I find that some people are genuinely forgetful when it comes to making payments, especially if they have placed their cake order months in advance. I always send out a reminder email for the deposit due the week that it is due. And if I come in on Monday morning and see that no deposit has been made, I give them a polite, but firm phone call, letting them know that if it is not paid before 5pm that day, their order is cancelled. It's good business practice to give customers a chance, however if you don't put an end date and a consequence, then there is no sense of urgency.

3. Be Clear

In your Terms & Conditions (you need to have these!), make sure you send them with each and every quote, and with invoice. And if you can, outline your payment terms on both of these documents also. Clearly state how much is owed, by when, and how the customer can make the payments. Whether it's in cash, direct transfer, credit card or PayPal.

4. Refunds & Credits

Again, this is where Terms & Conditions are essential. Have a clear procedure for refunds and credits. I always take a non-refundable deposit. If the customer cancels, I very well may have missed out on another order for the same week, so I do need to make up for this somewhere. However if they give me enough notice, I do offer them a credit towards their next purchase, in place of this from time to time. Have a clear outline in your head what you think is fair to your business and your customers, and again.. be consistent.

5. Use Of Tone

Whether you are contacting customers via email, Facebook, text or phone call. Make sure that your demeanor is always polite. Use a polite tone of voice. Re-read through your messages before hitting the send button. And if you have a frustrating customer. Take 5 minutes before replying to their 'unreasonable' request. With the use of a polite tone, but a firm business presence, this shows exactly how professional you are.

6. Keep In Mind, YOU Are The Business

Always keep in mind that you are the business. Most of us cakers are generally a one man/ woman show, and we deal with all aspects of the business. Remember that most businesses/ companies that have a make to order process, send out reminder and follow ups. It is professional to do this. It is also polite to send a friendly follow up, and it's also a form of being firm saying 'Hey... pay this please, otherwise your cake won't get made'. It is ultimately up to YOU to make sure that your customer pays the correct amount and on time.

IMPORTANCE OF COLLECTING DEPOSITS

(And how to make sure you get them)

One BIG cakey topic that is always going around in Facebook groups when cakers are asking for advice is 'Do you take deposits?' Or there is someone saying 'I've had a customer not turn up for their cake and I am now out of pocket.' Something along these lines.

In this section of the worksheet, we will be working on the importance of collecting your cake deposits, how much you are going to collect, when you are going to collect them by and how to make sure you get them.

After this, we will work on concreting these into your Terms & Conditions, and how the Terms & Conditions can be the back bone and life saver of your business come a complaint.

1. **Do you currently take a deposit for your cake orders?**

2. **How much deposit do you take, and when do you require the deposit by?**

3. **Do you feel like there could be improvements when it comes to your deposit terms, and if so, why?**

LET'S LOOK AT THE IMPORTANCE OF TAKING A DEPOSIT.

As cake decorators, we book in several cakes each week and sometimes we book them months in advance. We need to know exactly what orders we have coming up, booked and LOCKED in, that we will be doing so that we know our schedule, how many orders we can take, how much income we have for ourselves, and if we need any particular supplies/ingredients/packaging for our orders.

To bake and decorate our edible art means that we need to outlay money. And what's the use in outlaying money, if we are not going to be 100% certain that our order is booked in, and we are going to get a final payment from our customer?

Many cakers find themselves out of pocket because of this reason… not taking cake deposits.

Taking a customers cake deposit can help us with the following:
- Help pay for supplies to create the cake
- Makes you look more professional, as established businesses generally take deposits
- Concretes in the order – a paying customer is a serious customer
- Covers any $$$ spent, or orders we have knocked back, if the customer chooses to back out of the order (non-refundable deposit)

Some ways on ensuring you get your deposit:
- Have your deposit terms stated clearly in your T&C's, and attach to all of you quotes and invoices
- Keep your deposit terms the same for ALL customers, friends, family and general public
    - o *Note – I have different terms for businesses and general public*
- When you send an invoice, make sure you CLEARLY note when their deposit is due
- For last minute orders, make sure you have (and state in your T&C's) that deposits are due before close of business that day, or within 24 hours – whatever your prerogative
- Have a system that easily allows you to see who has deposits due when, and send out a 'deposit reminder' to anyone who has deposits due for the upcoming week
- Life get's busy, so if your customer doesn't pay after your deposit reminder, contact them again via phone call to discuss if they have any questions
- If you still don't get a response, give your customer an ULTIMATE deadline for payment and give them a consequence…. CANCELLATION of their order
- If you still don't get a response… cancel their order and notify them of this CLEARLY

It will VERY rarely get to the last action step, but it does happen.

LOOKING BACK OVER THE ABOVE–

When are you going to request a deposit by? (*7 days from invoice, 14 days before pickup, 1 month in advance...*)

How much deposit are you going to request?

When are you going to request deposits for last/short minute orders?

What do you consider a last/short minute order?

How much deposit/full payment are you going to request for last minute / short minute orders?

Write your terms CLEARLY below for your deposits (both normal and last/short minute orders):

When are you going to implement your new deposit terms and how?

TERMS & CONDITIONS

Having Terms & Conditions is a crucial part to running a successful business.

Having your business morals and values let customers know what you stand for and how you like to run the business. However having Terms & Conditions let customers know the non-negotiable factors of your business. That each and every order is subject to the same Terms & Conditions (unless otherwise stated), and the little particulars of your business.

Take a look at the Terms & Conditions template included.
This is an excellent starting point - simply enter in your business information and adjust any information or add / delete any of the sections that do or do not apply to you.

The template covers everything from your ingredients, through to cancellations and refunds. It is not as in depth as some Terms & Conditions provided by business, but it definitely has enough information, that if you have a conflict with a customer, you can refer to your Terms & Conditions and work something out that is fair for the both of you.

I would like for you to, either compare the sample to your existing Terms & Conditions, and see if you can add anything to your existing. Or if you have nothing at all, or very basic T&C's, use the sample and fill in your details
and change certain clauses, or add relevant clauses to your basic T&C's.

When are you going to put these implement your new Terms & Conditions and how?

Let's look at some specific ways to implement and concrete your new Terms & Conditions:

- Make sure you have your T&C's displayed clearly on your website, on your Facebook page notes section and anywhere else you see fit
- Whenever you make a big change or update to your T&C's, make sure you announce it, and let everyone know of the change, and whether it applies to existing orders or only new orders
- Make sure that you attach your T&C's to any quotes and invoices that you send to customers
- Be consistent. Treat every customer the same, and do not break your own T&C's. Remember that everything can be at the discretion of the owner, but best not to stray from your path unless absolutely necessary

So what are your next steps?

I invite you to believe in yourself and go forth and make your dream your reality! Take it one step at a time, and if you need more help, I'm here for you. Ask me questions and share your wins and struggles with me—I really do want to hear about your journey!

And if you want more support, here are some other ways we can work together:

- **Join Cake Biz Bootcamp**: This is my signature subscription-based online course. It includes workbooks and video tutorial lessons, plus personalized guidance to help you no matter where you are in your baking business journey. Visit https://cakebizbootcamp.com for more information.
- **Join my private Facebook group**: In this group, you can follow along with baking business tips, cake, and baking resources, and even ask baking-related questions. There are thousands of members from all over the world. https://www.facebook.com/groups/16761960292272616
- **Read my blog**: Visit https://angelfoods.net/ for free resources and recipes.
- **Listen to my podcast,** *The Cake Biz Broadcast: Sweet Snippets for Success.* I share frequent business tips for bakers, and I interview top baking industry leaders who share their stories. Visit https://thecakebizbroadcast.libsyn.com/ to listen, rate, and subscribe.
- **Follow me on social media** for pictures of my cakes and more business tips:
    - https://www.facebook.com/cakebusinessschool
    - https://www.facebook.com/snarkysweetcakechick
    - https://www.instagram.com/cakebusinessschoolllc/
    - https://www.pinterest.com/angelfoods
    - https://www.youtube.com/channel/UCqAUCprXWI70--ecqpeIVzg

Other Resources:

Software:

Convertkit: This is **a full-featured email service provider** (ESP). Thanks to its ease of use, automation, and other features, it's one of the fastest-growing email marketing companies around. It also offers customizable sign-up forms and landing pages to help bring in more email subscribers. Visit my affiliate link for a free 14 day trial: https://convertkit.com/?lmref=hbDgQA

BiziBakes: This is a service for a quick and easy website set up for your cake or baking business. Visit my affiliate link for more information here: https://bizibakes.com/ref/2/

BakeDiary: BakeDiary is the leading cloud-based software for cake decorators and bakers all over the world to help manage the admin side of your cake business. Visit this link to sign up and use code CBS15 for 15% off! https://www.bakediary.com/

Acknowledgments

I'd like to thank the following people who cheered me on while writing this book:

My husband, Jeff, who has been my biggest supporter and cheerleader in this journey.

My favorite business author, Mike Michalowicz, who inspired me to write.

My Cake Business Coach, Rebekah, who coached me through the process of pursuing my cake passion full time.

My Soul Coach, Stephanie, who helped me with my confidence and mindset.

My book support team, Jordan, Shelby, Patti, Samantha, Kerk, and all the amazing people at SelfPublishing.com, who helped with every step of the writing process.

And last, but certainly not least, my family and friends who have always been so gracious to listen to my rambling about all things cake!

Author Bio:

A former Accountant, Nicole Bendig-Lamb successfully turned her hobby of baking into a full-time gig as the owner of Snarky Sweet Cake Chick, LLC. She helps her clients create epic memories for their celebrations as a Master Cake Designer and Former Food Network Competitor. She also owns and operates Cake Business School, LLC where she educates and coaches other hobby & home-based bakers on the business side of baking. As a Certified Profit First Professional and Certified Fix This Next Advisor, she's got the skills and experience to help you with your sweet business dreams!

Can I Ask for Your Help?

Did you love this workbook? Don't forget to leave a review!Every

review matters, and it matters a *lot!*

I invite you to head over to Ingram Spark, Barnes & Noble, Amazon, or wherever you purchased this book to leave an honest review for me. This helps me make the next version of this book and future books even better:

Bakingyourwaytothetop.com/review

I appreciate your support!

–Nicole